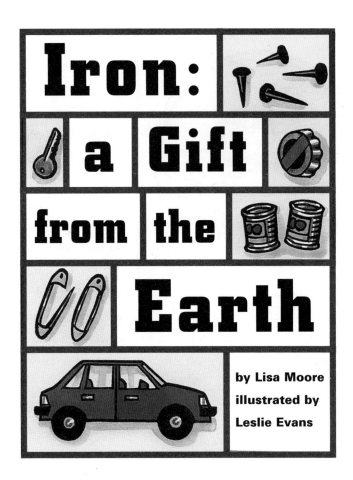

Iron: a Gift from the Earth

by Lisa Moore

illustrated by

Leslie Evans

Harcourt

Orlando   Boston   Dallas   Chicago   San Diego

Visit *The Learning Site!*

www.harcourtschool.com

Earth's Most Abundant Element

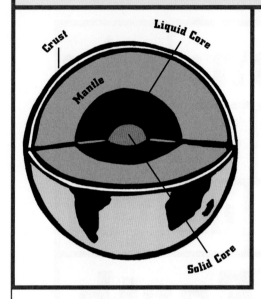

Did you know that ninety-two elements compose everything on Earth—including people, buildings, plants, oceans, and air? You have probably heard of many of these elements, such as oxygen, hydrogen, and nitrogen. Which element do you think is most abundant on Earth? You might be surprised to discover that iron is the element that occurs most often in a natural state on this planet.

In fact, 34.63 percent of our planet is made of iron, but you shouldn't start excavating your backyard looking for it. Most of the iron on this planet is in the Earth's solid core, located at the very center of the Earth, 6,371 kilometers below the surface. There is enough iron in the Earth's crust, however, to have made a profound difference in human lives—in modern times and throughout history.

Iron forms 5.8 percent by weight of the Earth's crust. This makes it the fourth most abundant element and the second most abundant metal in the crust. (Aluminum is first.) In addition, iron can be found in every state in the United States and in nearly every country in the world. Here are some facts about iron's abundance:

- More than ninety percent of all metal refined in the world is iron.
- People all over the world mine hundreds of millions of tons of iron ore each year.
- Machines made of iron produce almost everything we use.
- A survey by the United Nations after World War II estimated that there was enough iron to supply the world's demands for the next 800 years.

When it comes to people's use of metals, iron is clearly the most popular choice. People have been using iron to make practical and ornamental objects for more than 3,500 years, and, over time, methods of iron production have constantly improved as well as working conditions for those who mine and work with iron.

 While iron is plentiful on Earth, it is also abundant in many stars in our universe, including the sun. Iron really is "out of this world!"

The Iron Age

Greek Furnace

Although iron has been plentiful throughout history, it was not the first metal that people of the ancient world used. In about 6000 B.C., people in Asia crafted armor and tools out of copper and lead. By 3000 B.C., people had learned to make bronze by mixing tin and copper.

Experts believe the Egyptians were the first to use iron to make products that would enrich their lives. They made ornaments from the pure iron they found in meteorites between 4000 and 3000 B.C. Iron has two major advantages over copper or bronze—it is less expensive, and it is present in greater abundance.

Many centuries passed after people first used iron, before they learned to smelt it. Smelting means gathering ore, heating it, and separating the iron from the other materials in the ore to produce pure iron. The first people to smelt ore were the Hittites in about 1500 B.C. The Hittites lived in Anatolia, in the area of present-day Turkey. This discovery gave the Hittites a great advantage over their enemies, so they guarded the secret of iron smelting for as long as they could.

By 1000 B.C., the knowledge and technique of iron smelting had spread through much of Asia, Africa, and Europe. This time period marks the beginning of the Iron Age, the era in which people began to use iron for most of their tools and weapons. As populations increased, so did the number of machines—and the demand for iron.

Over the centuries, different cultures all around the world invented their own ways to smelt iron ore. Many kinds of furnaces were built that could hold fire hot enough to burn away certain elements and leave the iron behind. The Greeks made one kind of furnace, the Romans another, and the French another.

Of course, each culture improved the design. Furnaces became better and more efficient, and they produced more and more iron. The Catalan furnaces of Roman times produced about 150 pounds of iron in a day. The German furnaces of the Middle Ages could make about 150 tons of iron in a year. By 1756 in England, furnaces refined 100,000 tons each year. Furnaces today produce more than twice that much.

When did the Iron Age end? It hasn't. Iron is still used to make millions of products, from large, industrial machines to small, portable objects you might carry in your pocket. Think about the items in your world that contain iron: cars, trains, airplanes, and ships; washing machines, dishwashers, and refrigerators; hammers, nails, saws, and shovels; cans, keys, safety pins, and bottle caps. The list goes on and on!

Types of Iron

Iron is classified into three categories, according to how pure it is and how much carbon it contains. The three categories of iron are pig iron, wrought iron, and cast iron.

Pig iron contains about ninety-three percent iron. Pigs are bars of iron that each weigh about eighteen kilograms (forty pounds). Today, most pig iron is used to make steel. It is called pig iron because the bars used to be poured into molds gathered around a middle channel. The molds resembled a litter of baby pigs snuggled around their mother.

Wrought iron is nearly pure iron. It can be hammered into various shapes when it is heated. It resists rust better than cast iron. Wrought iron is durable, strong, and elastic, but not very hard. This is the material that a blacksmith heats in a forge to hammer into various shapes.

Cast iron cannot be shaped at any temperature. It is manipulated by pouring liquid iron into molds and letting it harden. Its hardness, low cost, and strength make cast iron suitable for huge beams and other construction materials. Fine cast iron is so hard it can cut diamonds.

Sources of Iron

When found in the Earth's crust, iron is never pure; it is always chemically combined with other elements. The term *iron ore* refers to minerals with enough iron to make them worth mining. Here are six examples:

- *Hematite* and *magnetite* occur when iron combines with oxygen and contain about seventy percent iron. Hematite can be black, brown, or dark red. Magnetite is black and also magnetic, making it easy for miners to locate.
- *Limonite,* or bog ore, is iron combined with water. It is yellowish brown and can be as much as sixty percent iron.
- *Pyrite* is about half iron and half sulfur. Its shiny gold appearance has earned it the nickname "fool's gold."
- *Siderite* is a gray-brown mineral of about 50 percent iron, found primarily in England and Germany.
- *Taconite*, about 30 percent iron, is a hard rock that contains specks of hematite or magnetite. As deposits of richer iron ores are used up in the world, deposits of taconite are in greater demand.

Iron, the Element

The chemical symbol for iron is *Fe*, which derives from the Latin word for iron, *ferrum*. Iron has an atomic number of 26 and an atomic weight of 55.85. It melts at 1,535°C and boils at 3,000°C. Iron reacts with water and air to form rust and is easily magnetized.

The Earth's deposits of iron ore are layers of rock and minerals under the Earth's surface. To reach and mine the ore, miners either open up the surface to expose the whole layer or dig down into the layer and bring the ore back to the surface.

Most of the world's large deposits of iron ore were formed by geological processes that began millions of years ago. In shallow seas, iron in the salt water settled to the bottom. There, it formed blankets of iron-rich rock. Later, thanks to earthquakes and gradual shifts, this rock rose above the level of the water. These deposits can be extensive. For example, iron ore deposits in the Hamersley Range in Australia are 1,000 meters thick and span an area of about 200,000 square kilometers.

Other iron ore deposits are *igneous*. This means that they were formed when volcanoes poured lava, high in iron content, onto the Earth's crust. The rich iron deposits in Sweden, South Africa, and in the province of Quebec in Canada were formed in this way.

As mentioned before, miners use two methods to get iron ore out of the ground: open-pit mining and tunnel mining.

To create an open-pit mine, miners first strip away the surface layers of earth with enormous excavation machines. Next, they use explosives to loosen and break up the ore. Then, huge power shovels scoop the ore into trucks or railroad cars for transport to mills where the ore is processed.

Most of the world's iron ore is extracted from the Earth through open-pit mining. In the United States, about ninety-six percent of all iron ore is mined this way. You might see one of these mines as you drive along the highways across the United States. Open-pit mines are sometimes carved into the sides of mountains.

The largest open-pit mines in the world are near Lake Superior, in Minnesota and Michigan. These mines supply about eighty-five percent of the iron ore consumed in the United States. They extend over many square kilometers and are as deep as 500 meters.

Tunnel mining is necessary when iron ore deposits are deeper underground. First, miners dig tunnels into the deposit. Then, they enter the tunnels to remove the ore. Mining companies install conveyor belts or use special railroad cars to move the ore to the surface. Sometimes, miners drill horizontally into the slopes of mountains. Because tunnel mining is more hazardous and expensive than open-pit mining, it is used only in places where there is a rich deposit of top-quality ore.

The graph below illustrates the leading iron ore mining countries in the world. Each symbol on the graph represents 20 million tons of ore.

Leading Iron Ore Mining Countries 🛒 **20,000,000 tons**

Usable iron ore mined in one year (1995)

China	🛒🛒🛒🛒🛒🛒🛒 🛒🛒🛒🛒🛒🛒
Brazil	🛒🛒🛒🛒🛒🛒🛒🛒🛒🛒
Australia	🛒🛒🛒🛒🛒🛒🛒
Russia	🛒🛒🛒🛒
United States	🛒🛒🛒🛒
India	🛒🛒🛒
Ukraine	🛒🛒🛒
Canada	🛒🛒
South Africa	🛒🛒
Venezuela	🛒

Making Iron

You could say that smelting iron is like baking a cake, only the product is heavier and not nearly as tasty.

From the kitchen of Vulcan:
Vulcan's Favorite Iron
1 1/3 tons of iron ore
3/4 ton of coke
1/4 ton of limestone
4 tons of air
Preheat furnace to 3,500°F. Add iron ore, coke, and limestone together until iron ore melts and all impurities have been removed.

Factories that produce iron use enormous ovens called *blast furnaces*, which are cylinders of steel lined with heat-resistant bricks. Some blast furnaces rise higher than a fifteen-story building from foundations that are more than 30 feet wide. Blast furnaces get their name from the steady blast of air forced into the bottom to produce the heat that melts the ore.

Iron workers load iron ore, limestone, and a coal by-product called coke into the top of the blast furnace. These ingredients are called the *charge*. When the charge hits the blast of hot air in the furnace, the coke ignites, burns, and melts the iron. The tremendous heat in the lower portion of the furnace—more than 3,000°F (1,600°C)—causes the raw materials to liquefy. As the materials become liquid, their volume decreases, creating room for more raw materials to be added. The melted iron settles to the bottom, and every four or five hours, liquid iron is collected into huge cars through taps at the base of the furnace. Rugged iron workers tap up to 400 tons of molten iron at a time.

11

Once a blast furnace has been ignited, workers keep the fire burning until the brick lining begins to deteriorate. The lining lasts about two years. Iron and steel mills churn around the clock. Across the United States and all around the world, blast furnaces burn incessantly, feeding iron to a hungry world.

Iron mills must keep their furnaces clean to make sure they burn properly and safely. If the furnaces work efficiently, they produce more than just iron; almost every iron by-product is marketable. The leftover liquid from the burned rocks, called *slag*, is used to make cement and building materials. Some of the waste gases are pumped back into the furnace itself, and others are used to make steel. Even the smoke contains worthwhile chemicals used in fertilizers and other products.

The First American Iron Mill

The first iron mill in the United States was built in the 1640s in Saugus, Massachusetts, about ten miles north of Boston. The mill produced about 150 tons of iron a year. Today, the mill is a historical monument where visitors can pay tribute to an important part of America's industrial history.

From Iron to Steel

Some people think of steel as another kind of iron, like cast iron or wrought iron. In fact, steel is made in steel mills from purified pig iron combined with other metals to make *alloys*. Steel is harder and stronger than iron and can be transformed into millions of serviceable objects.

When making steel, carbon is removed from the iron. Then a furnace heats the iron until it liquefies, after which different elements are added. Steel companies produce thousands of varieties of steel. Adding various elements gives steel different characteristics. A single car may have 150 varieties of steel installed in its body and engine! Here are just a few examples.

- *Nickel steel* is tough and resistant to stress. It's used in the manufacture of bridges, towers, and bicycle chains.
- *Tungsten steel* is used in cutting tools that must stay sharp, even at high temperatures.
- *Manganese steel* can hold up under high impact, so it is ideal for huge earth-moving shovels.
- *Stainless steel* is made by adding chromium to iron. Because it can get wet again and again and never change its appearance, it is used to make flatware.

Recycling Iron and Steel

Have you ever seen a junkyard full of scrap metal? You might have noticed towers of cars, dishwashers, refrigerators, garbage cans, and metal pipes—all made of iron and steel that people have discarded. These are more than mountains of junk, however. Scrap metal can be used to produce new iron.

Scrap metal is a valuable part of the iron-making industry. Factories must treat scrap metal to remove everything that isn't iron or steel. Paper, rubber, and plastics can be eliminated by burning them off. Iron can be separated from other metals, because each metal melts at a unique temperature. When the process is finished, you cannot distinguish between brand-new iron and recycled iron.

For this reason, the reuse of iron and steel is one of the world's most successful recycling stories. Consider how much energy humans save by not having to mine and smelt more iron ore. To help save the environment, don't throw away that bicycle or hubcap or wrench. Recycle it instead.

Effects on the Environment

To produce iron and steel, factories also create a certain amount of pollution, but there are laws to keep damage to the environment under control. For example, when mills make iron and steel, they produce a number of toxic or hazardous gases. Laws require that the chimneys of furnaces have dust catchers, spray chambers, and other cleaning equipment. Often, the gases and smoke are trapped before they enter the atmosphere and are then recycled as fuels.

Vast quantities of coal in the form of coke are used to make iron and steel. Coal is one of the Earth's fossil fuels. It has been estimated that the world's supplies of coal will last only another 300 years.

Most people in today's world depend upon iron and steel. However, many environmentalists pose the question: Is it worth the hazards to our environment to meet this ever-growing demand?

Iron: It's Everywhere

More than any other metal, iron represents durability and abundance. It is all around us—in our land, in our tools, and even in the cells of our bodies.

The average human body contains about 3.5 grams of iron, most of which is in the form of *hemoglobin*. Hemoglobin transports oxygen from the lungs to the rest of the body. Because your body must contain iron to be healthy, be sure to eat iron-rich foods, such as fortified cereal and green leafy vegetables. If a person's body is iron deficient, he or she suffers from a condition called *anemia*. Anemia results in extreme weakness and fatigue.

Rudyard Kipling, a renowned British writer and poet, composed a poem called "Cold Iron." His lines of verse are a tribute to the most abundant element on Earth. Here is an excerpt.

> *Gold is for the mistress—silver for the maid—*
> *Copper for the craftsman, cunning at his trade.*
> *"Good!" said the Baron, sitting in his hall,*
> *"But Iron—Cold Iron—is the master of them all."*